The Art of Framing

By Charlene Brown

This book includes everything an artist or collector needs to know to mat and frame all types of artwork (oils, watercolors, acrylics, prints, photos, etc.) — from choosing the mats to cutting multiple mats with multiple windows, constructing shadow mats for three-dimensional objects, arranging and attaching the items in the frames, building a shadow box frame, making fabric-covered mats, and creating faux finishes.

WALTER FOSTER Publishing, Inc.
430 West Sixth Street
Tustin, California 92680-9990

Contents

Introduction

One of the questions most commonly asked when it comes to framing is, "Is it cost-effective to do it myself?" This is, I believe, based on the misconception that 'framing' consists solely of building the frame. Actually, that is only a minor part of the whole project. In the past framing has generally involved a basic rectangular frame with a rectangular mat, but this isn't true anymore. Framing and, particularly, matting have become an art in their own right. And, regarding the question of cost-effectiveness, considering that a major portion of the cost for framing goes toward the labor-intensive assembling, the answer is yes! Of course, there is no way I can judge the value of your time, but if you are a creative person, I assume you want as much creative control over the finished project as possible. The best way to achieve that control is to do your own framing.

One notion I would like to dispel is that you have to buy a large quantity of expensive tools to do your own framing. This simply isn't true as you will see in the step-by-step section of this book. While some people enjoy woodworking and prefer to build their own frames, I recommend that you buy them pre-cut and pre-assembled from a quality frame supplier. (I also recommend buying pre-cut framing glass.) **Read the step-by-step section for both projects before you begin.** This will prevent frustration and save the expense of buying tools or supplies you do not need.

There are many factors that affect framing and as a creative person you are probably familiar with many of these considerations. However, rather than dedicating pages and pages to subjects such as color, I have chosen to concentrate on framing and matting. If you would like more information on color, I recommend *Color (And How To Use It)* by William Powell from Walter Foster's Artist's Library Series.

The projects herein will demonstrate everything you need to know to mat or frame almost any type of artwork. In the step-by-step sections you will see what appear to be rather complicated three-dimensional projects. Don't let this discourage you as they are much simpler than they look. *Note — You can use these instructions to frame two-dimensional pieces as well.*

If you have any questions or want a special frame and mat combination don't hesitate to consult a framing shop. One of the shops I worked with when writing this book, The Artisan Frame and Gallery in Tustin, California is happy to spend time helping their customers choose frames and mats, even if the customer plans to doing the framing themself. The framer's expertise and exchange of ideas is incredibly valuable.

Most importantly, this book gives you the chance to make framing and matting a more creative part of any art or collectible. As you begin your projects, relax, enjoy the process, and remember that patience is a special virtue when it comes to framing. Good luck! You should find these projects very rewarding!

Materials

NOTE—YOU PROBABLY <u>DON'T</u> NEED <u>ANY</u> OF THESE TOOLS!

Before you purchase any materials, read through the instructions in the step-by-step sections of this book. You may need only a few of these items for your project—or none at all.

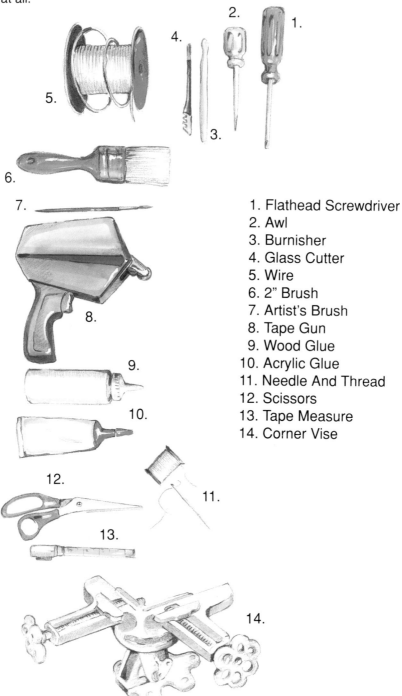

1. Flathead Screwdriver
2. Awl
3. Burnisher
4. Glass Cutter
5. Wire
6. 2" Brush
7. Artist's Brush
8. Tape Gun
9. Wood Glue
10. Acrylic Glue
11. Needle And Thread
12. Scissors
13. Tape Measure
14. Corner Vise

The most expensive part of professional framing is the design and the labor. You can save money by doing these things yourself—and **YOU DON'T NEED TO BUY ANY EXPENSIVE TOOLS!** Simply purchase a pre-cut mat and a pre-assembled frame, then put them together yourself.

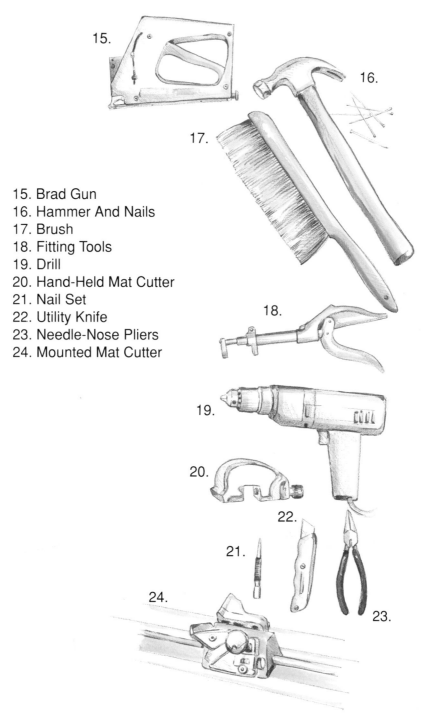

15. Brad Gun
16. Hammer And Nails
17. Brush
18. Fitting Tools
19. Drill
20. Hand-Held Mat Cutter
21. Nail Set
22. Utility Knife
23. Needle-Nose Pliers
24. Mounted Mat Cutter

Choosing the Mat

Many people assume that the main purpose of the mat is to enhance the artwork by adding texture and color. But, actually, the primary purpose of the mat has been to protect the artwork by keeping it flat and preventing the glass from touching it. The mat creates space between the art and the glass so humidity will not collect on the artwork. If humidity does get on the artwork and the artwork is pressed against the glass, the artwork may transfer or "offset" onto the glass, removing the image from the surface of the art. In the worst cases, mold and/or a white film can form on the artwork — a devastating and costly experience.

Traditionally, the "rule of thumb" for deciding whether or not to mat and glaze (cover with glass) a particular piece of artwork depended on the surface used; i.e., if the work was on paper it was matted and glazed; if it was not on paper (such as an oil painting on canvas) it wasn't matted and glazed. This rule is not true anymore, especially for mixed media and specialty papers. Also, the matting is fast becoming an intricate part of the finished art. So, once again, we find there are no firm rules with art.

There is a large variety of styles, colors and textures of mats. To aid you with basic terminology that will help you describe what you are looking for we have prepared the following diagram.

1. Faded Cream Neutral Linen Mat
2. Blue Marble Mat
3. Double Mat with V-Groove
4. Double Mat withGold Fillet
5. Black Leather Mat
6. Black Core Marble Mat
7. Pewter Silk Mat
8. Fabric White Linen Liner
9. Acid-Free Mat Board
10. Simulated Grass Cloth Covered Mat
11. Linen Fabric Mat
12. Silk Fabric Mat
13. Triple Mat
14. Desert Suede Hand-Covered Mat
15. Burgundy Double Mat
16. Black Linen Mat

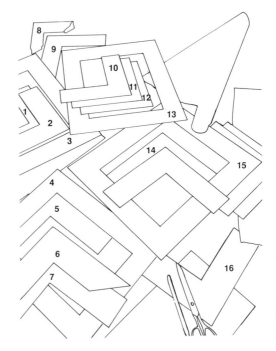

Choosing the Frame

There are several basic principles to consider when selecting a frame. However, these are only suggestions — there are no firm rules with art.

(1) A period frame should match the period of the artwork. And, following the same concept, the frame should parallel the art; i.e., light, frivolous work is best suited to a frivolous or fanciful frame; a bold graphic piece goes best with a bold frame such as a solid colored, high gloss frame. A obvious misuse of this principle would be to frame a folksy painting, such as a red barn, in a metal frame rather than a rough wood frame. (2) The thicker the artwork, the thicker the frame; i.e., a stretched oil painting is thicker than a watercolor and the frames usually follow suit. While this was originally done because sturdier frames were needed to hold the heavier works, it has now become standard. (3) When framing pastels or other pieces susceptible to smudging, you may want to choose a frame thick enough to accommodate a spacer (see Glossary) instead of a mat. (4) It is generally believed that frames which slant toward the artwork actually enhance the depth of perception and draw the viewer's eye into the work. (5) White frames and mats often darken and flatten the art, which makes white an unpopular color.

There is an infinite number of mat and frame combinations. And while you may be able to go to a store and choose from a group of samples, there is some basic terminology that will help you describe what you are looking for. For this reason we have put together this diagram, both to show examples and to give you ideas.

1. Country French Frame with Gold Design
2. Cherry Finish Traditional
3. "Queen Victoria" Embossed Light Sand with Gold Highlight
4. Gray and Black Marble with Gold Lip and Back
5. Antique Gold with Black Back
6. White Faux Marble with Gold Lip and Gold Line on Edge, Satin Luster
7. Blackest Black Lacquer Molding
8. Classic Gold Shadow Box
9. Standard Black Metal
10. Champagne Silver Metal
11. Rock Gray Faux Stone Metal
12. Antique Silver Compo Design
13. Gray Metal
14. Deep Red Faux Burl with Gold and Black Lips
15. Hand Painted Black and Pastel Floral with White Wash Lip and Back
16. Blue-Gray Wash with Gold Lip and Antique Gold Wash
17. Pickled Pine Acorn Carved and White Washed
18. White Washed Compo Design/Ready-made with Beige Velvet Liner

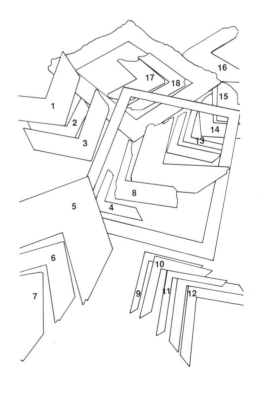

Project 1: Shadow Mat Frame

This project is made up of multiple mats, multiple windows, shadow mats, and two- and three-dimensional pieces. It may appear difficult, but if you follow the instructions carefully you should find it quite easy.

The step-by-step format is designed to aid you from start to finish — from matting to glass cutting to framing and all steps in between. **The project shown here may involve more complicated matting and framing than you need for your piece, but the instructions are designed to be used for simpler projects as well. Just follow the steps you need and skip the rest.** For example, you may need to know how to cut multiple mats but not how to construct shadow mats, so simply bypass the steps for constructing shadow mats. (Be sure to read through the instructions before you begin so you will know what materials you will need.)

Note — When making a shadow mat frame the arrangement of the pieces is critical. There are no right or wrong compositions in art; however, there are general guidelines you may find helpful. For example, it is generally accepted that horizontal art or arrangements are soothing, while vertical arrangements are usually considered more confrontational. (This is probably because of our upright position and our peripheral vision. Note that TVs are horizontal.)

Select the items you would like to frame. You can make a shadow mat frame for just about any subject, occasion, or object: weddings, anniversaries, coins, sports, births, miniatures or other collectibles, etc. Also, decide if you want to use one frame or a series of frames.

Selecting the Mats

Choose mat colors that go well with the collection of items. Gold, metallic gold and navy were used for this piece because of the flat gold of the tassel, the metallic gold of the printed items, and the navy blue of the tassel. (The mats are shown here, already cut.)

Note — You do not necessarily have to match the items; sometimes contrasting colors are the best choice.

Mat Cutters

There is a wide variety of mat cutters available. The table-mounted type was used here, but you can use any kind you are comfortable with. Table-mounted cutters are more expensive than the hand-held type, but they are easier to work with.

Note — There are special cutters available for cutting oval or circular windows.

An unmounted hand-held cutter is shown here. For best results, use a straight edge as a guide.

Note — Some framers use these types of cutters for free-style cuts.

Here is another type of unmounted hand-held cutter. Notice the angle of the blade; this creates the beveled edge of the window.

Note — While it is preferable to hand-cut the mats, it may be more economical to buy them pre-cut as mat cutters can be relatively expensive. Quantity and artistic control will be the deciding factors.

Arranging the Pieces

Arrange the items you plan to frame. Once you are happy with the composition, lay the pieces on the back of the top mat (blue in the example). Because you are working on the back of the mat, you will have to reverse the position of the items so that whatever is on the right side will be put on the left, etc.

Use a pencil and a tape measure to mark where the corners of the items are.

Note — You may want to wear cotton gloves when handling original artwork or photographs.

Cutting the Mat

If you are using pre-cut mats, go to step one on page 16.

Draw guidelines for the windows. Use a measuring tape, a t-square, or a ruler to make the lines straight and the corners square.

Note — When cutting the top mat you will need to allow ample space around the items so that when you get to the bottom mat, where the windows are smaller, the items will still fit in the openings.

Follow the instructions from your mat cutter to cut the windows. Rather than cutting each window individually, cut the vertical lines of each window first. (This will prevent you from becoming confused and cutting the wrong lines.)

Turn the mat sideways and cut the horizontal lines of each window. If any corners are still attached, cut them with a razor blade — don't tear them loose or you might damage the mat.

Note — It is better to undercut each window and finish with a razor blade than to overcut the lines.

When all four sides are cut, pop out the piece of mat (the "fallout"). Save the fallout to use later.

This is an example of what happens when you overcut a window.

Note — You can use these instructions for framing any type of artwork — watercolors, oils, acrylics, photographs, posters, etc.

If you overcut the window you may be able to repair it by gently burnishing over the cut. Use an artist's burnisher or a smooth piece of wood or plastic to gently burnish over the cut mark until it is barely visible.

To measure the windows for the second mat, lay the top mat over it and trace around the inside of the windows with a pencil. Remove the top mat, then measure and draw new guidelines slightly smaller than those from the top mat. Do the same for the bottom mat, making the windows even smaller.

Note — Some people prefer to cut the bottom mat first, then the windows in the other mats are made larger.

The windows in the middle mat are 1/4 inch smaller (1/8 inch on each of the four sides) than those in the top mat. The windows in the bottom mat are 1/2 inch smaller (1/4 inch on each of the four sides) than those in the top mat. Follow the instructions from pages 13 and 14 to cut the windows.

Note — When you cut the bottom mat, make sure the items still fit in the windows.

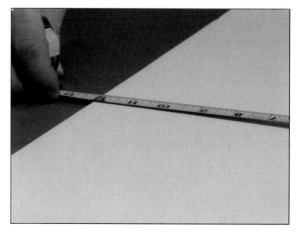

Attaching the Mats

Apply double-sided tape to the solid areas of the bottom mat with a tape gun (or by hand). Don't place the tape too close to the windows or it will show.

Place the middle mat on top of the bottom mat, centering the mat carefully so each window has equal borders. Smooth the middle mat down with your hands so it will adhere to the bottom mat.

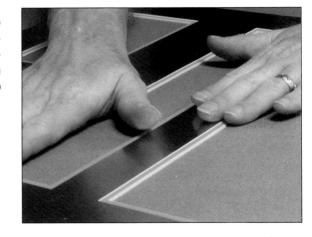

Use double-sided tape to attach the top mat to the middle mat. Make sure the windows are even on all four sides.

Note — You can use these instructions for matting individual pieces of art — just cut one window.

Once the mats are secure, lay the items in the windows to check the sizes and positions. It is much easier to correct or start over now than after you have added the shadows and the backing board.

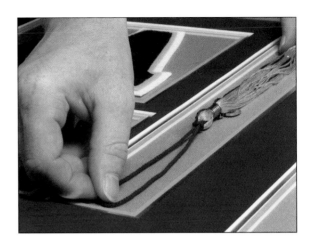

Shadow Windows

The three-dimensional pieces need shadow windows. Measure the width and length of the windows that are for three-dimensional objects. To determine the depth, measure the depth of the largest item and make all the shadow windows large enough to accommodate it.

Note — The shadow windows in the example are all 1/2" deep because that is what was needed to fit the depth of the tassel.

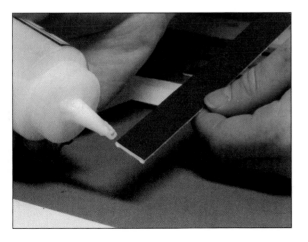

Measure and cut strips of mat to fit around all four sides of each shadow window (in the example the shadow mat is the same color as the top mat). The strips in the example are 1/2" wide which is the depth of the shadow mats, as explained above. Apply glue to an edge of one of the strips.

Note — Be sure to use a glue that dries clear.

Place the strip as close to the window bevel as possible without overlapping the bevel. Hold it in place until the glue sets.

Note — The front side of the mat should face toward the open window.

Repeat the process with all four sides of each shadow window. Hold each piece until the glue sets. Make the sides straight and place the edges close together to make the corners.

Put some glue on the corner seams, then reinforce each corner with masking tape. When the glue is completely dry, remove the tape.

Put glue around the top edge of one of the shadow mats.

Note — Be sure to use glue that dries clear.

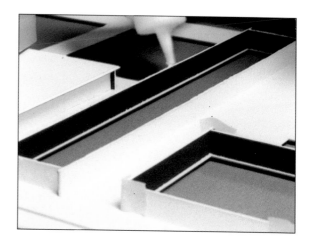

Carefully place the backing on top of the shadow window. (Use the fallout from the window of the top mat.) The front side of the mat should face down. Hold the backing in place until the glue sets. Repeat this process until each shadow window is complete.

When you turn the mat over it should look something like this.

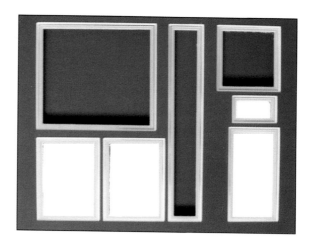

Attaching the Pieces

Lay the pieces in their respective windows. Use silicon glue or another adhesive that will not damage the items to attach them. Obviously, if the items are irreplaceable you may want to use something other than glue. Read the label on the glue before before applying it.

Carefully place the items in their windows and press them down so the glue will adhere.

Note — You can use these instructions for framing any type of artwork — watercolors, oils, acrylics, photographs, posters, etc.

When glue will not hold the item well enough or you choose not to use it you may need to sew the item into place. Use a tape measure to make sure the item is placed exactly as you want it because the needle (obviously) leaves holes in the mat.

Use a needle and matching or "invisible" thread to attach the item. Take your time and try to hide the stitches as best as you can.

Some items may need a combination of thread and glue. This pin had to be poked through the mat when it was attached.

Place a piece of tape across the tops of the flat items for placement in their respective windows. (Cloth or strong packing tape works well.)

Place the items in the windows. After each piece is attached at the top, check the placement. If the positions are satisfactory, tape the remaining three sides.

Reinforcing the Mat

To reinforce the mats, foam board is used to build up the back of the windows that do not have shadows. Measure the recessed areas.

Cut the foam board to fit the spaces, then glue several layers of foam board to the back of each window until they are approximately the same depth as the shadow windows.

Assembling the Frame

If you are using a pre-assembled frame, go to step two on page 25.

It is strongly recommended that you buy pre-cut frame moldings. Use wood glue to attach two pieces of molding in an "L" shape and place them in a corner vise.

Note — It is easier to make two L-shaped pieces and then combine them for the final frame than to add the third and fourth sides to the first L shape.

Make sure the corners fit well by running your fingers over the seam. (This is critical as it is extremely difficult to fix once the glue has set.)

Wipe any excess glue off the corner with a lint-free cloth. Let the glue dry completely.

Note — You can use these instructions for framing any type of artwork — watercolors, oils, acrylics, photographs, posters, etc.

Reinforce the corners with finishing nails. Use an electric drill to make small holes in the places where you plan to put the nails. There are two nails in each corner of the example.

Note — You may use a nail for the drill bit, but some framers prefer to use a bit slightly smaller than the nail.

Hint: An old carpenter's trick is to lightly tap the point of the finishing nail with a hammer to prevent the molding from splitting.

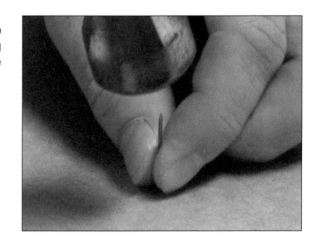

Gently drive the nails in with a hammer.

Note — It is best to place the nails on the bottom and the top of the frame so they will be less noticeable.

Recess the nails into the frame with a nail setter. Repeat this process with the other L, then attach the two L's together. Fill the nail holes and any gaps in the corners with putty that matches the frame.

The Framing Glass

It is recommended that you buy the framing glass pre-cut. If you choose to cut your own, measure it then cut it with a glass cutter, as shown. Break the extra pieces off carefully. Once you become skilled at this, you can lay the glass over the mat and cut it.

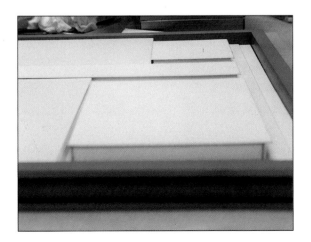

Clean the glass with a non-ammonia cleaner, then place the glass and the mats in the frame.

Note — The artwork should never touch the glass. Use spacers to keep them apart, if necessary.

25

The Backing Board

Measure and cut a piece of acid-free illustration board or foam board for the backing board (the backing board fits inside the frame). Use a brad gun to fasten the backing board to the frame.

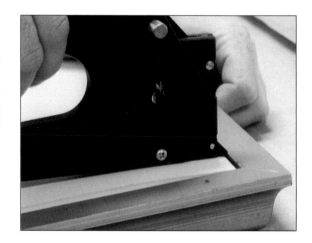

Alternative: If the mats or the artwork are disturbed by the movement of the brad gun you can use a fitting tool such as the one shown here.

Apply double-sided tape around the back of the molding with a tape gun (or by hand).

Place brown craft paper over the backing board, letting it stick to the tape on the molding. Carefully trim off the extra paper with an art knife or a razor blade.

Attaching the Hanging Wire

Measure down from the top of the frame about one-third of the way and mark each side of the molding with a pencil.

Use an awl to start holes for the eye screws over the pencil marks.

Screw in the eye screws.

Note — This is the best way to hang heavy frames. There are "picture hangers" available for lighter pieces.

Hint: After the eye screws are started, use the awl to screw them in the rest of the way.

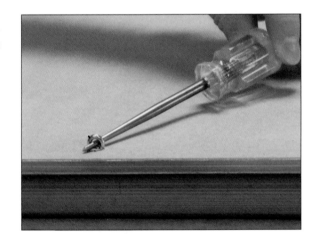

Thread wire through the eye screws and twist the end of the wire around itself, as shown.

Be sure to leave some slack in the wire for hanging.

Place rubber bumpers on the bottom of the back of the frame. The bumpers will keep the frame away from the wall.

The Shadow Mat Frame

Here is the completed frame. As you can see, it was much easier to assemble than it appeared in the beginning.

Note — You can use these instructions for framing any type of artwork — watercolors, oils, acrylics, photographs, posters, etc.

Project 2: Shadow Box Frames

 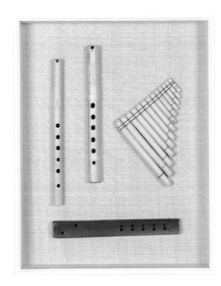 

This project demonstrates how to make shadow box frames with cloth-covered backing mats. As with the first project, it may appear difficult, but if you follow the instructions you will find that it is not.

We begin this project with frame construction. We will assume you have already selected the items you wish to frame, the molding and the cloth that will work well with the collection of items. Because of the "folksy" nature of the items used in this project we selected a natural fabric.

Decide if you want to make one frame or several frames. A series of three frames was used for these travel keepsakes

Assembling the Frame

If you are using a pre-assembled frame, go to step one on page 34.

Place wood glue on two corners of the frame. Put the pieces together and make sure they are lined up well.

Place the L-shaped piece in a corner vise.

Note — It is easier to make two L-shaped pieces and then combine them for the finished frame than to add the third and fourth sides to the first L-shape.

Make sure the corners fit well by running your fingertips over the seam. (This is critical as it is extremely difficult to fix once the glue has set.)

Wipe any excess glue off the corner with a lint-free cloth. Let the glue dry thoroughly.

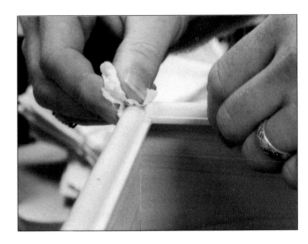

Reinforce the corners with finishing nails. Drill small holes where you plan to put the nails. There are two nails in each corner of the example. If you place the holes on the bottom and the top of the frame they will be less visible.

Note — You can use a nail as the drill bit, but some framers prefer to use a bit slightly smaller than the nail.

Gently tap the tips of the nails, then drive them in with a hammer.

Note — You can use these instructions for framing any type of artwork — watercolors, oils, acrylics, photographs, posters, etc.

Recess the nails into the frame with a nail setter. Repeat the entire process with the other L and then attach the two L's together.

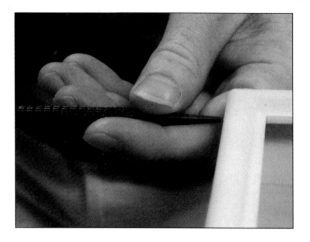

Fill in the nail holes with matching putty. Before the putty dries, wipe off any excess with a lint-free cloth.

Fill in any gaps in the corners with matching putty. Before the putty dries, wipe off any excess with a lint-free cloth.

The Framing Glass

Measure and cut a piece of glass (or buy it pre-cut). Once you become skilled at this, you can lay the glass on top of the frame while you cut it. Clean the glass with a non-ammonia cleaner and place the glass in the frame.

Note — The glass should never be allowed to touch the artwork.

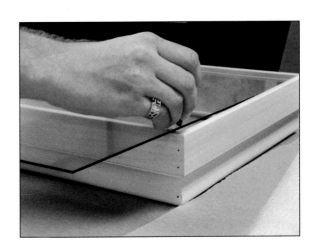

Covering the Mat Boards

Measure the depth of the frame, then cut long strips of foam board or mat board to fit. (Each frame needs four strips.)

Note — The material shown here is professional framing cloth. You can find many types of cloth at fabric stores, or you can order from a framing supplier or frame store.

Apply glue to one side of each foam board strip and carefully place them on the material. Smooth the strips down with your hands or a rolling pin.

Note — There are several kinds of glue that can be used; read the labels. (Spray adhesives can also be used, but they may have health and environmental risks.)

Let the glue dry thoroughly, then use scissors or an art knife to trim the extra material off the strips.

Use a mat cutter or an art knife to cut the strips to the proper lengths to fit inside the frames.

Apply glue to the backs of the strips. Spread the glue evenly.

Note — You can use these instructions for framing any type of artwork — watercolors, oils, acrylics, photographs, posters, etc.

Place the strips inside the frame and hold them in place until the glue sets (this should only take a moment).

Measure and cut a piece of foam board for the backing board.

Put glue on the foam board and cover it with fabric. Use a rolling pin to smooth it out.

Use scissors to cut the cloth off the roll. Let the glue dry thoroughly.

Use an art knife or a razor blade to trim the extra fabric off the board.

Arranging the Pieces

Position the items on the cloth-covered backing board. Try different arrangements until you are satisfied with the composition.

Attaching the Pieces

Attach one of the items to the board with silicon glue or another adhesive that will not damage it (read the label). Hold the item in place until the glue sets. Obviously, if the items are irreplaceable you may want to attach them with something other than glue.

Carefully position and attach the remaining pieces.

Note — You may want to wear cotton gloves when handling sensitive artwork or photographs.

If necessary, use straight pins to hold the three-dimensional pieces in place while the glue sets.

When glue will not hold the item well enough or you choose not to use it, you may need to sew the piece in place. Be sure the item is placed exactly as you want it because the needle will (obviously) leave holes in the mat.

Use a needle and matching or "invisible" thread to attach the items. Take your time and try to hide the stitches as best as you can.

Sew where needed for position or extra support.

Note — You may want to wear cotton gloves when handling sensitive artwork or photographs.

The Backing Board

Close the frame and use a brad gun to nail the backing board to the frame.

Alternative: If the items are disturbed by the movement of a brad gun, use a fitting tool such as the one shown.

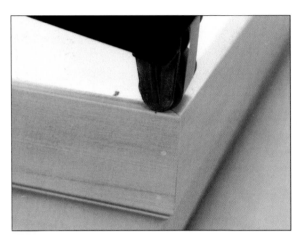

Apply double-sided tape around the back of the molding with a tape gun (or by hand).

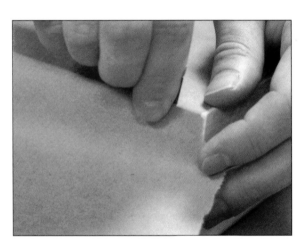

Place brown craft paper over the backing board, letting it stick to the tape on the molding. Carefully trim off the extra paper with an art knife or razor blade. Follow the instructions on pages 27 through 29 to attach the hanging wire.

Shadow Box Frames

This is an excellent way to frame any type of three dimensional object.

Note — You can use these instructions for framing any type of artwork — watercolors, oils, acrylics, photographs, posters, etc.

Fabric Covered Mats

To recycle an old mat or just to create a warm, decorative effect you can cover a mat with fabric, wallpaper or other specialty papers. Fabric is used in the example.

Apply fabric glue to the front of the mat. Make sure the glue is spread evenly, then roll the fabric over the mat. (You can also use spray adhesive, but it may have health and environmental risks.) Smooth the fabric down with your hands or a rolling pin. Cut the fabric off the roll.

Measure 1-1/2" in from the window of the mat and make guidelines with a pencil. This extra material will wrap around the inside of the window.

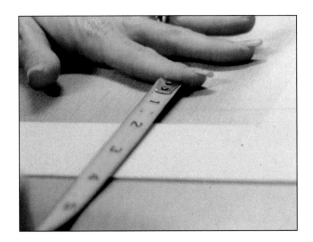

Use a razor blade or an art knife to cut the window out of the fabric.

Pull the center fabric free from the window.

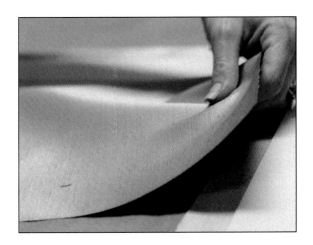

Use a razor blade or an art knife to cut diagonal slits in the fabric from all four corners of the mat.

Apply double-sided tape around the window on the back side of the mat.

Wrap the fabric around the window. Pull it tightly and stick it to the tape.

Smooth the fabric down with your hands. Make sure there are no wrinkles on the front side. Check each side before going on to the next.

Reinforce the corners with masking tape, as shown.

Trim excess fabric from the outside of the mat, then you are ready to proceed with framing.

Faux Finishes

There are many techniques that can be used to recycle old, discolored, or mismatched frames and mats such as the ones shown on page 43. You can paint or refinish frames, or you can cover mats with fabric or wallpaper (see page 46). A marbleizing effect was used on the mat and frame shown here. For special effect finishes such as this you may want to buy a kit. (A kit will save you from having to buy large quantities of materials.)

When doing any type of refinishing, it is better to apply several thin coats than one thick coat. Let each coat dry for at least an hour — follow the directions on the label. You may need to apply more than one coat to cover the frame completely. Various shades of green acrylic paint were used for this project.

Creating a Marble Effect

This brown wood frame and neutral colored mat were transformed into the unique "marble" frame shown above.

Sand the frame with a #220 grade sandpaper or steel wool and wipe the frame clean. Then use a 2" brush to paint the frame with acrylic paint (a medium shade of green was used for the example).

While the frame is drying, carefully sand any frayed edges in the mat window with a very fine (#220) sandpaper or an emery board.

Use a small sponge or crumpled plastic wrap to dab a second color on the frame and the mat (dark green was used for the example). If necessary, you can remove some of the paint with a crumpled paper towel.

Before the paint is completely dry, put the frame and the mat together and use an artist's burnisher (or similar tool) to score the "marble" lines on them. Drag the tool over both pieces in continuing strokes.

Use a small artist's brush to fill in the scored "veins" with white acrylic paint. You may want to use a stiffer brush to blend the veins. Separate the mat and frame and allow them to dry thoroughly.

After the mat and frame have dried, put them back together and paint them with a clear acrylic varnish to protect them. Apply several thin coats of varnish rather than one thick coat.When the varnish has dried you are ready to proceed with framing.

Arranging the Finished Artwork

The artwork, the frame, and the mat are not the only important parts of a piece — the placement and the arrangement are just as significant. As an art collector, I find that the most attractive homes and offices are those which have been decorated around the art; i.e., when the art has been considered before the color of paint, the wallpaper and even the furniture. To get the most from your art, consider the following guidelines.

The presentation of the artwork is often as important as the piece itself, especially when the piece is potentially for sale. **When hanging art, one must consider color, texture, direction, and subject**. For example, I would not hang the proverbial "red barn" painting in an ultra-modern room; nor would I hang high-tech graphics in a traditional Country French setting. Also, people will often hang a piece of art regardless of the room setting just because they have the art and there is a blank wall. The result is generally a miss-match that detracts from both the art and the room and cheapens the whole look.

Once the subject and its relationship to the room have been taken into account, one should consider color and texture. Rather than buying artwork to match the furnishings, most collectors prefer to consider the artwork first, and then choose background colors to compliment the art. Texture is a similar consideration. Color and texture can be used either to highlight a portion of the art or to compensate for it. For example, to create a dramatic effect, one might place a striking frame (of course, it must work with the art) against a dark wall. (Note — dark walls and highly-stylized frames will create a dramatic effect, but they will not offer the warm feeling that many people want in their homes.) Decorators often use these dramatic effects in the entry or on one wall of a room. They can then balance the rest of the room with warm colors and textures. Remember that some of the dramatic effects that look so good in a gallery or a magazine can grow tiresome when you see them everyday.

To create a decorator look with texture and color the artwork should be considered before the wall. In other words, if you are redecorating a room, first choose the pieces you feel will collectively represent the feeling you want to achieve in the room, then choose the wall color or wall covering. Decide where you want to hang the pieces. Remember, you do not have to paint all the walls the same color, although selection must be done tastefully and subtly. For example, choose a common tone from the art (i.e., a particular cream color) and use the color as a base color in the paint and/or the wallpaper to enrich the entire room. It is disheartening to discover after you have painted that the yellowish of the wall paint detracts from the art. Think this through before selecting the wall paint. Ideally, if you are going to use wallpaper and paint, you should try to find a common (subtle) color from the art, the paint, and the wallpaper. When possible, the draperies and the furniture should also be a part of this overall plan. Finding a common color/tone is easier than you may think. Don't forget to work the mats into this equation; they can help tie everything together. You may even be able to use the upholstery fabric to cover the mats.

Direction is an important factor when determining the placement of the art within a room. Basically, remember that the human mind will follow the eye. If a painting has a road that leads to the horizon, the eye will follow the direction of the road. What the eye finds at the end of the road is up to you. As a general rule, do not hang a directional piece where it will point toward a door or a window. (This will cause viewers to stare out the window.)

It is better to have the directional lines point toward another piece of work or to the center of the room. Take advantage of direction to steer the eye into something impressive, such as another piece of art, a fine piece of antique furniture, a piano, or a sculpture.

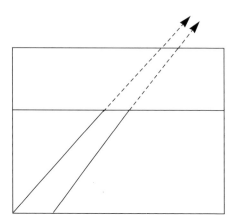

Directional

Note — Another thing to consider when placing artwork is sunlight. **Direct sunlight can fade the artwork, so avoid hanging your art opposite a window.**

Also, remember to consider the size of the artwork in relation to the wall space. Put a medium size work on a medium size wall, a large piece on a large wall, etc. Otherwise, you will dwarf either the wall or the art.

One of the best ways to tie a group of pieces together is to use coordinating mats. For example, you can use mats covered with the same kind of material, but in different colors. The subtlety of using silk mats in different colors, for instance, will not be consciously picked up by the viewer, yet will subconsciously tie them together.

Collector's Tips:

1. Don't hang artwork just "because it's there."
2. Consider the size of the art and the room.
3. Match the subject of art and the style of the room.
4. Wall coverings and wall color should be selected to accent the art.
5. Keep art away from direct sunlight.
6. Disconnected groupings need a more rigid arrangement.
7. Ornate frames should be placed on plain backgrounds while dramatic effects may be created with dark backgrounds.
8. Use one of the recommended methods for grouping artwork (see pages 51 - 53).
9. Stair step arrangements are not recommended.
10. Remember that horizontal arrangements are more soothing while vertical arrangements are more engaging.
11. Watch for direction in art and use it to your advantage.
12. Remember, these are only guidelines — there are no set rules.

Groupings

There are three basic ways to group artwork: *the grid, the flush-edge,* and *the centerline.*

The Grid — The grid is used for strongest appeal, especially when it is necessary to overcome inconsistences in the items grouped. (For example, a collection of small, unrelated prints.) In unrelated frames such as those found in Country French decor, the grid technique is the best choice. This is because weaker pieces need a stronger arrangement to create the feeling of belonging. For a grid pattern, measure the wall into sections, then place the art at the cross sections. Focus the cluster in the center to draw the viewer in.

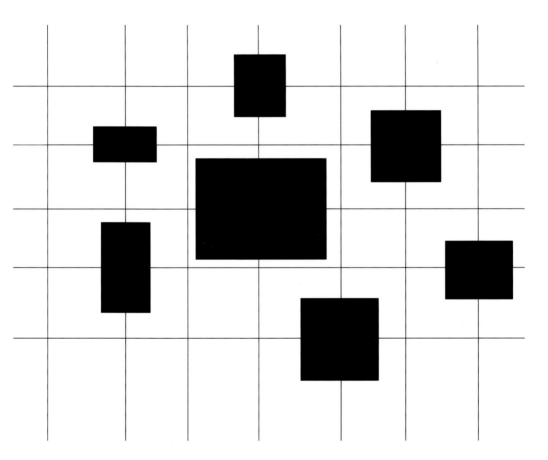

The Grid

The Flush Edge — A common technique used in galleries is the flush edge. This gives an appearance of formality and importance, although it may not be the best way to draw the viewer in. For the flush edge, a height is selected (i.e., the top of a window or an arbitrary measurement such as 18 inches down from the ceiling), then the tops of the pieces are all hung at that height.

The Flush Edge

The Centerline — The most popular method for non-cluster arrangements is the centerline. For this technique, the centerlines (or horizon lines) of the pieces are lined up horizontally. (Don't confuse the centerline with the center of the frame.) Refer to the diagram below. Notice that the centerline is rarely in the center of the picture.

Usually, if no furniture is against the wall the guide for the centerline is 5-1/2 feet from the floor. When furniture is present, the bottom of the frame should be at least a foot above the furniture. Also, for each additional foot the viewer will normally be away from the art (as in a large room), the art should be raised one or two inches. Once you determine the centerline focus, hang each piece on the imaginary guideline. This is the most popular way to hang two paintings next to each other.

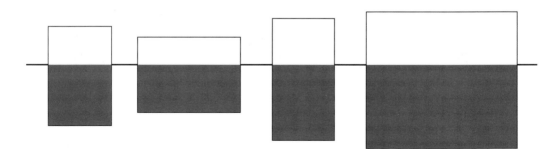

The Centerline

The Stair Step — The stair step technique is not recommended as it is generally considered ineffective. It is too distracting and is difficult to follow. The straight vertical or straight horizontal methods are much stronger. The grid technique can be used to accomplish these arrangements.

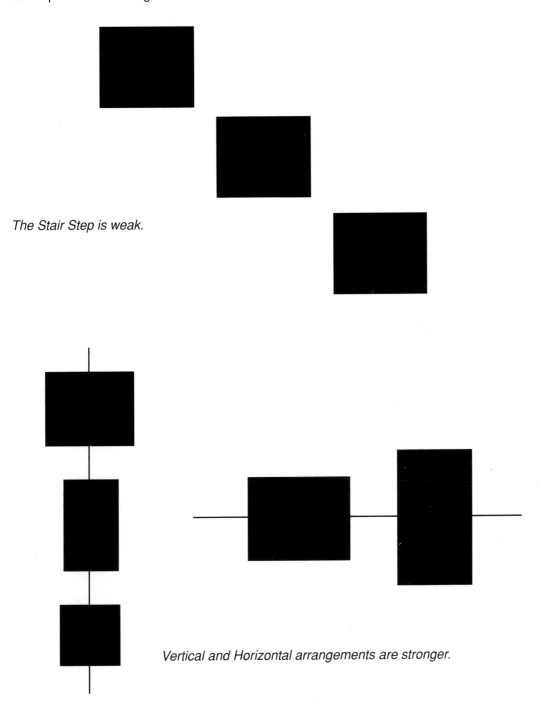

The Stair Step is weak.

Vertical and Horizontal arrangements are stronger.

GALLERY

"Never Just Black And White" by Chris Hensley Watercolor 24" x 36"
Black and white wood frame with black and grey acid-free mats. Multiple windows and cutouts.
Framed by: _The Artisan Frame & Gallery,_ Tustin, California

"Candy Bowl" by Lance Fogel
Watercolor 19" x 19"
Octagonal white lacquer frame with
white and green acid-free shadow mats.
Framed by: _The Artisan Frame & Gallery,_
Tustin, California

"Airplane, Train, Car and Ship"
by Lance Fogel
Colored Pencil and Pastel 27" x 34"
Natural flat ash frame; artwork
floated on cream linen fabric mat.
Framed by: *The Artisan Frame
& Gallery,* Tustin, California

"Journey's End" **by Chris Hensley Ink and Watercolor 39" x 32"**
Rounded pastel-washed wood frame with triple black core matting; Sante Fe-style cut.
Framed by: *The Artisan Frame & Gallery,* Tustin, California

"Panda" by Marilyn Grame
Watercolor 17" x 21"
Black lacquer frame; green
and black acid-free mats.
From Walter Foster book
#222, _Animals In Watercolor._
Framed by: _The Artisan Frame
& Gallery,_ Tustin, California

"Peony and White-Crested Laughing Thrush" by Lucy Wang Watercolor 31" x 24"
Black and white faux marble frame with gold lip inside and outside; artwork
floated on acid-free burgundy mat with gold fillet and white linen outer mat.
From Walter Foster book #233, _Watercolor On Rice Paper._
Framed by: _The Artisan Frame & Gallery_, Tustin, California

"Red-Tailed Hawk" by Gene Franks
Pencil 20-1/4" x 16"
Black matte-finish frame; black, dark
grey and light grey acid-free mats.
From Walter Foster book
#231, *Animals In Pencil*.
Framed by: *The Artisan Frame
& Gallery*, Tustin, California

Oriental Fan 14-1/2" x 20-1/2"
Antique gold frame with
blue velvet backboard.
Framed by: The Artisan Frame
& Gallery, Tustin, California

Graduation Shadow Mat Frame 21" x 36"
Blue lacquer frame with black suede, gold, and navy blue
suede mats; eight flat openings, three shadow mats.
Framed by: *The Artisan Frame & Gallery,* Tustin, California

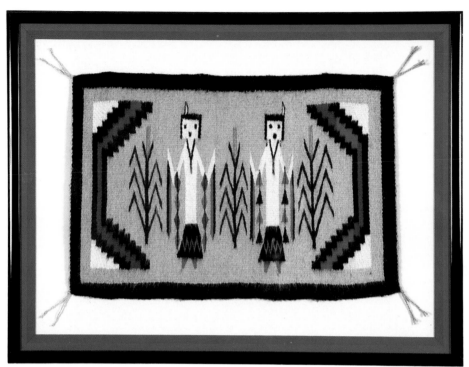

Navajo Rug 27" x 56"
Black laquered frame with white linen backing
mat and red cloth-covered corner mat.
Framed by: *Partners,* Laguna Niguel, California

"Yei Be Chai Dancers of Winter" 13" x 13"
Rough wood frame with a spacer
and glass for protection.
Framed in-house

American Song Festival Award 13" x 15"
White metal frame; white and gold mat boards; spacer.
Framed by: *Concept Framing,* Laguna Niguel, California

"Portal"
by Michael David Ward
Mixed Media Lithograph
48" x 48" x 47"
Translucent red
wood frame; three
multiple-angled mats.
Framed by: *The Artisan
Frame & Gallery,*
Tustin, California

"Peruvian Street Scene" 30" x 46"
Weaving stretched over wood artist's frame.
Framed in-house

**The J. Paul Getty Museum,
Simone Martini,** *"St. Luke,"*
1330s, Oil, 22-1/4" x 14-1/2"
Hand-carved frame.
Used with permission

**The J. Paul Getty Museum,
Franz Xaver Winterhalter,**
***"Portrait of Leonilla Furstin zu
Sayn-Wittengenstein-Sayn,"***
1843, Oil, 56" x 83-1/2"
Hand-carved gold leaf frame.
Used with permission

The J. Paul Getty Museum, Gentile da Fabriano,
"Coronation of the Virgin," ca. 1420, Oil, 34-1/2" x 25-1/2"
Hand-carved gold leaf frame.
Used with permission

Glossary

ACID-FREE — Paper materials that have a ph factor above 7.0. Acid-free papers have no sulfur or other contaminants that can mix with humidity to deteriorate the artwork.

AGATE — A stone used for burnishing gold leaf onto frames.

ALKYD-BASE PAINT — A basic paint used for frames. It can be colored with oil paints.

ANTIQUING — A finishing effect (sometimes using pitting) to create the appearance of age.

APPLIQUE — A cutout decoration applied on a frame or mat.

ASPHALTUM VARNISH — An absolutely black varnish which contains asphalt.

BACKING BOARD — The cardboard, foamboard, chipboard or other material used in the back of the frame to keep the mat and artwork secure.

BACK SAW (Miter Saw) — A saw with reinforcement on the dull side of the blade. This aids in control while cutting a molding in a miter box.

BEADING — A thin piece of wood (generally gold leaf) used to decorate frames. The beading acts as a frame within a frame.

BEVEL (Beveled Edge) — The angled cut edge of the window in a mat.

BLANK — A mat cut to the size of the frame but without windows.

BOLE — A rarely used type of clay that is placed between the gesso coat and the gold leaking with the intent that it show through where the gold leaf is distressed. It is available in a variety of colors.

BOX FRAME — A frame that is a box with glass sides to display heavier objects such as sculpture. A box frame should not be confused with a shadow box frame which is a window deep frame generally used to frame three-dimensional pieces of art and craft items.

BURNISH — To rub with a wood or plastic tool (called a burnisher) to compact or smooth. (Note that agates are used for burnishing gold leaf.)

CENTERLINE (Horizon Line) — An imaginary line that runs horizontally through a piece of art. One method of hanging art in a grouping is to line up the centerlines of the pieces.

CLUSTER — To hang pictures in an informal grouping.

COMPOSITION — The arrangement of any collection or individual subject matter in art (i.e., compositional direction refers to art that has purposely been focused in one direction such as the left, right, etc.) Another commonly used term is "compositional balance," referring to the composite feel of a piece of art.

CONSERVATION BOARD — An acid-free mat board generally used for valuable art. This mat board which contains rag or chemically treated wood pulp is preferred by most museums and professionals.

COUNTER DIRECTION — In groupings, the use of a variety of directional works which counter each other.

COVERED MAT — A mat covered with fabric, wallpaper, suede, etc.

CRAFT PAPER — Brown waxed paper used to cover the back of a frame or to wrap framed art for transport.

CUT — The finished size of a mat.

DECORATIVE ART — A term generally used to describe functional art.

DISPLAY — An arrangement or collection of artwork.

DISTRESSING — To indent or recess a frame to create the appearance of the aged nicks found in antiques.

DOCUMENTARY CARD (Insurance Card) — A certificate with pertinent information about a particular piece of art. It should be kept in a secure location in case of fire, theft, etc., along with a photograph of the piece.

DOUBLE MAT — Two mats used together. The windows are generally cut so the window of the top mat is 1/4 to 1/2 inch larger all the way around so the bottom mat shows.

DOUBLE HANGING — Hanging two similar pieces of art together.

DRY MOUNTING — A heat process of attaching two pieces (generally a mat board and a picture) together using adhesive. Strengthens and flattens the art work or photo.

EYE LEVEL — The height common to most people's eyes. When hanging art at eye level there should be compensation for perception; i.e., for each foot the viewer is away from the art, the art should be raised one to two inches.

FALLOUT — The piece left over after cutting a window in a mat.

FAUX FINISH — An artificial finish; painting or staining techniques to create the appearance of marble, wood, etc.

FILLET — A strip of wood, plastic, or mat separating the mat, glass and/or artwork.

FINISHING NAILS — Slender nails with virtually no head which can be recessed into wood (the frame).

FLOATING FRAME — A frame with the impression that the artwork is floating — generally accomplished by leaving a space between the frame and the art.

FLUSH EDGE — A method of hanging art so either the top or bottom edges of the pieces are lined up with each other. This is especially effective when the works have a particular relationship to each other.

FOXING — Rust or mildew damage on artwork.

FRAME — An open structure built and joined together with the intent of holding and outlining artwork.

GESSO — Chalk or gypsum whiting mixed with animal hide glue. Gesso is used over wood or canvas to prepare it for painting. Gilded finish, gold leaf or another finish created by burnishing a thin layer of gold leaf material or other material on top of a frame.

GILDING — The process of applying paper-thin gold leaf or a similar finish to a frame.

GLASS CUTTER — Tool similar to a knife used as a knife to cut glass.

GLASSINE — A storage material similar to wax paper. It is placed between stored works of art for protection.

GLASS MAT — A piece of glass used in place of a mat. Actually artwork is placed between two pieces of glass.

GLAZE — (1) To finish a frame with varnish or other shiny coating. (2) To cover artwork with glass.

GLAZIER — A person who fits glass into frames.

GOLD LEAF —Traditionally, paper-thin strips of real gold applied on a frame. (Artificial gold leaf is also available.)

GRID PATTERN — A method of displaying art where the horizontal and vertical lines intersect which makes the arrangement easy to follow with your eyes. The grid pattern is often used in interior design by aligning artwork with the wall lines.

GUIDE BAR — A mat cutter bar that guides the knife when cutting mats.

INERT — A substance that will not cause chemical burning because of its chemical neutrality.

LINER — The bottom mat in a frame.

MARBLEIZING (Marbling) — Creating a faux (artificial) finish that looks like marble.

MARQUETRY — To inlay decorative patterns into the wood veneer of a frame.

MAT — A pressed cardboard or conservation board which is used to accent and surround a work of art.

MAT CUTTER — A tool for cutting mats. There are two different types: one is hand-held and angled approximately 60° against a guiding board; the other is attached to a bar which is secured to a table.

MITER — The beveled angle (usually 45°) on the end of a piece of molding where a joint is made by fitting two angled pieces together.

MITER BOX — A box with guides for handsawing a miter joint at the proper angle (not recommended for accurate and fine finished frames).

MOLDING — Rabbeted wood or metal strips from which the sides of the frame are cut.

MONOCHROMATIC — Artwork that is primarily one color using only black or white to create various effects.

NAIL PUNCH — A screwdriver-shaped tool used to recess nails into the frame.

OVAL — A mat with an elliptical or egg-shaped window. It also refers to an elliptical-shaped blank.

PICKLED WOOD — A frame molding with a special finished light effect which is created by adding a thin coat of white paint or similar finish.

QUADRANT — A molding with a quarter-circle profile.

RABBET — The recessed groove or cut on the back of a frame that supports the artwork and the mat.

RAGGING — A technique using a rag to create a distressed effect on a frame while the paint or stain is still wet.

RAG PAPER MATS — See acid-free mats.

REVERSE FRAME — A frame that slants away from the artwork.

SCORE — To create a crease in an area which makes it easier to bend or cut. Also, in the faux marble finish the veins were scored before painting.

SHADOW BOX — A deep frame designed to display three dimensional objects. Not the same as a box frame which is actually a box with glass sides to display heavier objects such as sculpture.

SPACER — A piece of cardboard, matboard or plastic used to create a floating effect in the mat or the frame.

SPRAY MOUNT — An aerosol glue which, while effective and convenient, is not recommended because of potential health and environmental risks.

ULTRAVIOLET (UV) LIGHT — Light rays with wavelengths shorter than visible light and longer than x-rays. Ultraviolet light is beyond the violet rays and invisible to the human eye. UV light comes from sunlight and fluorescent light (as well as other types of lighting), and can cause permanent bleaching damage to artwork.

UNDER MAT — The mat used as the placement mat or the bottom mat.

VEINING — A technique that re-creates the line patterns found in marble.

VISE — A tool used to clamp frame joints together while gluing, hammering, etc.

WINDOW — The opening in a mat where the art shows through.

Closing Thoughts

I would be remiss not to mention the other aspect of protecting you art — this time in the financial sense rather than the physical sense — which is maintaining documentation for insurance purposes. Document cards should be kept on all works as a standard part of framing and maintenance. Collectors and artists should get in the habit of labeling the back of the framed work. And, most importantly, you should have a set of records of your work or your collection which is kept separately from the artwork. I keep a small three-hole binder (or photo album) that does not easily fit in my safe deposit box, so I duplicate the records and send the copies to a member of my family. Keeping the records and the artwork in the same place is risky because of fire, theft, or floods. Record keeping is an important part of the framing for insurance purposes as well as for posterity.

I want to reiterate the recommendation for buying pre-assembled frames and pre-cut mats. I am sure you now know what I meant when I said that constructing the frame was only a minor part of the project. There is so much more to creating a framed art project. I hope you enjoy giving the frame and matting the attention your project desires.

I also want to remind you that if you have any questions don't hesitate to consult a framing shop. The Artisan Frame and Gallery in Tustin, California is happy to help their customers choose frames and mats, even if the customer plans to do their own framing. The framer's advice is extremely valuable. If you cannot find a frame shop in your area willing to help, you may want to consider mail order.

Good Luck!

Acknowledgements

I would like to thank all the people that helped on this book; their patience and cooperation has been incredible.

While I was able to do most of the photography myself, I am continually indebted to photographer, John Raley from Costa Mesa, California for his professional guidance. Also, John shot the cover, the mat and frame collages on pages 7 and 9, and most of the Gallery.

As always, I want to thank the staff at Walter Foster Publishing, Ross Sarracino, president, and, especially, Sydney Sprague, editor, who patiently answered my "what if I did this?" questions and is always thorough and wonderful to work with.

There were a number of consultants on this project, particularly my brother, Gary who patiently demonstrated how faux finishes were created, as well as other tips he has learned from many years as a custom painter and refinisher.

I want to give a very special credit to the J. Paul Getty Museum for providing the classics for our use. And, in the same sense, I want to acknowledge all the artists, weavers and craftpersons, including my artist partner of many years, Carolyn Davis.

Finally, and most importantly, I want to thank the framers who patiently held still and let me take over their work spaces while I photographed every minute step of their work: Suzanne Canfield and Edward Bushman of The Art Store in Newport Beach, California; John "Woody" Reagan; and, especially, the "framers extraordinaire," Ron and Cathee Goodis of The Artisan Frame and Gallery, 13721 Newport Ave. #6, Tustin, California.

Thank you all!